Top 20 Social Media Marketing Tips

Table of Contents

Introduction

Conclusion

Introduction

I want to thank you and congratulate you for downloading the book. This is will help you to know about social media marketing, importance and use social media for marketing and business, a list of top 20 social media marketing tips, the importance of social media tips for small business etc. This book will also provide the process of using social media and advantages of social media in our day to day life.

Chapter 1

What is social media marketing?

Social media is like an umbrella which describes the several activities that add technology, social communication, along with the creation of words, pictures, audio, and videos. When that is tasty, it does not initiate to express the radical changes of social marketing and networking.

The social related media has converted a social wonder which spreads into most social relations. Moreover, social websites have grown into a very powerful communication of free websites wherever people share their thoughts.

This is an internet marketing strategy in the retiring of terms which influences the power of sites like Facebook, YouTube, Twitter, LinkedIn, MySpace, etc. to form traffic in a website and build such website's online status. Thus, you are mainly doing social media marketing when you are posting a link to your website on Facebook, or tweeting.

The social sites are the most powerful matters of online. They can take social networking fast on Facebook. This has above half a billion listed users in the world. Only, it is the site to reach this kind of numbers and that is for Facebook. Therefore, you would never overlook and mistake the power of social media. It can be very slow but it is fully useful to anyone. You can certainly drive thousands of web traffic to your website by using social media if you can play your cards accurately. There are thousands of webmasters who are doing it, on an everyday base.

Advantages of social media marketing

The small businesses are looking forward to getting many customers and they must refer to social media marketing as it will allow them to bring more customers in locally and globally. Most of the consumers unite with different brands by social media and so a manager needs to make a website with a strong media company in the social world. It will help you to blow the interest of the possible consumers. Your businesses are probable to receive amazing success which will allow it to grow another level of performance when media marketing is applied efficiently. The benefits include:

1. **Many platforms:** There are various social media platforms when you are getting started in your business. These all seem to offer alike services with small changes and means of getting your favorite customer attention. Though, they fit into 3 classes: image-based, word-based, and video-based stages. But, a few of these classes become overlap. There are separate differences among the audiences which each platform spreads though there are similarities among a few of the numerous channels. The viewers have often chosen a certain social media network. All business must have a certain sort of consumer, and supply to that customer over their marketing and branding. It is more valuable for your business and brand development to spread onto many social media.

2. **The increase of traffic from niche talks:** Social media marketing will let your website to acquire volumes of traffic from niche dialogs that are gained through social networking websites, groups, thoughts, and blog comments.

3. **Improved brand consciousness:** The brand consciousness is recognized by your client base as many people visit in your website, seeing your business name, logo, and links to your site.

4. **Improved Search Engine Optimization:** The increasing of high-quality links to your website and blogs raises your SEO.

5. **Established belief:** People finish up gaining trust in your business through natural influences and relations that grow in online communities.

6. **Better visibility:** There are many people who will be appealed to your website because they try to search for keywords associated with your industry. The active contribution in social world will help you to keep the status of your business by proper communication with your customers and replying to their complaints.

7. **Successful campaign:** There are many good, fun cases to be found online if you doubt about the profits, as well as how it can help your business. There are one of the largest successes in 2013 that are rotated about three mobile and their turning pony. The campaign was founded on a television advertisement about a Shetland pony moonwalking over the scenery to be completed by Fleetwood Mac those actually taken viewers' attentions. The

advertisement finished with flashing the attention online and over social media. The video went viral immediately, and customers utilized their hash tag over and done with Facebook and Twitter. Video went up on YouTube, and reached 1.5 million views in the first week, and now it has grown about 10 million viewers. Three Mobile's campaign involved a second part that was wholly online and turned about their Pony Mixer and dressing up your own pony by selected a song for the pony to dance.

The making a good sign for your business needs that you will give the campaign face. You need there to answer questions, to view conversations as well as to post comments that will catch the attention of people. Businesses make a unit in the marketing department for social marketing.

Chapter 2

How to use social media for marketing and business?

You will not be astonished to see people from different age groups are playing with their tablets, laptops, and also for phones. This type of generation has become helpless to the internet for their wants. These days has gone when the internet is set generally for research and you can shop and order for food through online. Due to the vast popularity of the internet, big and small businesses have been using the internet to raise their businesses. Several of them have learned how to use social media for marketing.

Social media is most likely the most effective tools for marketing that are offered for business owners. Another method of media marketing is blog marketing and it is clear of making interest to your own web page by means of going to social networking sites.

In fact, blogging is easy, cheap, and absolute to be synonymous in today's online generation. An essential advantage of blogging is that you can certainly present your company's modern product. You can subtly present a new product or service deprived of telling your readers to the reward of the product. You can write in the blog in what way a consumer's problem was resolved due to availing your latest product or service.

Social media marketing would not come through like a press release. You must try to establish a connection with your readers before presenting your products and services in a blog. The creation of a stable relationship with your consumers is essential when you want to help a loyal habit. Blogs work efficiently in supporting your business, to give out flyers because people walk on the streets. Actually, you are not certain if the people are getting the flyers just throw them away as waste.

These blogs can be used as other social networking sites; you can make links to these social networks to your web page or blog. In fact, you have to make certain that you have an eye-catching blog and you use planned keyword content so as to exploit search engines. There is one reliable strategy that is to submit a blog article to sound article directory sites. These article directory sites will make links to your business's web page; therefore, it will help you in page ranking. You get to reach more people within a few mouse clicks with this marketing strategy.

There are some tips to use social media for your business:

- Social media is like a means of transportation to build your business. On the other hand, it is not sensible to sell from your social media pages. Most of the people will cooperate with you when they feel that you have some amazing information. You can give tips and advice to them to fed up with you if you try to sell directly. You need to visit your blog or website, and from there start to move from just being social media links.

- The best method to get somebody from your Facebook page or Twitter page is to excite them for free information which they can get if they go to your blog or website. There you would have decided that they need to fill their name and email address to get the permitted data when they get. You can send them more quality content with promotional material which you can start making money from when you have taken their email addresses.

- It can be wondering to you that which sites you would use to sponsor your business. There are many sites that you can use, but I will choose five that I think are crucial to your ongoing success. I must use Facebook and Twitter, where you are almost aware of extremely popular and will be able to get the best benefit from YouTube that is most useful because this site has billions of hits per year. If will be able to use it in the correct method, you can get hundreds of visitors to your website daily. I can use LinkedIn that is the big hitters in the internet marketing field and would copy some very essential links from many business professionals.

- You would not visit as a sales person in any way when you are balancing with people on social media sites and making your contacts on these pages. Talk about those people who use these sites to find information, exchange people and make friends. They must not go there intended for some heavy sales patter. Therefore, you must be pleasant and useful to people to build up their trust by showing interest in them.

- There are groups on many sites where you can join. You need to search for groups that are directly or indirectly related to your form of business. You can join with people, give them advice, useful data, and usually make many contacts with people that might be interested in offering for your business when you have joined these groups.

- You need to make friends and it is considered as the first thing. You can do this by only getting to know new people who are in the same industry. You can catch people whom you like and appreciate their work. On Facebook, this is as easy as sending them a 'Friend request'. The easiest thing is just to follow that person on twitter. The following for somebody on Twitter will not get you in difficulty with the law. Tools are available to set up your replies freely to follow someone when they decide to follow your friend. It became some confusing if you are bound for using this to drive traffic. You have got to set up some methods for doing nothing.

- Value is the same than anything we have talked about earlier. They are already attentive if somebody is following you with your friend. You can use Facebook page to ads your product. It is a certain way for people to eliminate from their list and for others to ignore your posts. Rather tells me, you would be confused and sometimes turned off. You need to know people formerly you accept that they would be a good fit your business. It is a method that takes some time. You can post links to your blog and those posts are giving relevant content as well as deliver some value.

- Personable Facebook is mainly a place for people where we can know about anyone. Somebody can have seen an article of yours blog post about your industry and they go to Facebook to get a good idea about you. It can be being an industry where your product isn't in the right choice. Thus, keep to a sign tune that is useful and is mixed with some current events of your life. You will gain knowledge of how to use social media to build your business because you spend more time and see more people for whom you admire to work. You need to get out there and make some friends to provide people with valuable content and you will have this social media for working in your favor.

Chapter 3

Importance of social media marketing strategy

The social media marketing strategy is based on social networks and interacting sites that is one of an essential tool for any internet marketer. The aim after the fact is very few things that have been able to show themselves actual than social networks. It can offer a large number of involvements which is useful for all internet marketers. Social media marketing strategy is the best way of linking with people and increases them on your contact list. The straight website created is not capable of doing it as rapidly as social networks can do. The best examples are to prove this is Twitter. Here, you will start getting information around a person's life, business, and other deeds. Therefore, isn't the firmest method of connecting with someone? Email cannot ever do this so fast.

You will get certain rules in social media marketing strategy and it is all internet marketers need to follow. The first and most essential rules are not to hire it over your personal brand. The social media is one kind of tool for your marketing strategy and it will not be used by itself. There is another important point that is never being violent. When somebody refuses your request, just forget about rejoining with them.

You must find a valuable message where your voice is on your social media marketing strategy. Sometimes, as an internet marketer, people will follow you if you offer them some valuable information. You need to work as an industry leader, a niche professional and provide expert tips and advice to your followers. Your social media marketing strategy must not contain one-sided sales areas. Try to know the fact that most of the successful internet marketers offer a platform for open discussions and message.

When you have proven a good follower on your social media marketing strategy, this is very significant to update it. People never branch about to your site when you do not have all new things to offer. This is an essential point of social media marketing strategy for all internet marketers. You must add your social media usernames on your website, blogs, E-Mails, and other tools of social media marketing strategy to run updated and repetitive information because people always remember updated information.

You must maintain a balance among your personal and expert life. Keep both hundred miles apart than any kind of information that imitate your personal views, be it pious and share your personal life would be kept far from your expert network.

Social networks are a very active tool of social media marketing strategy for all internet marketers which are the importance of conservative tools because these applications and skills are fairly new, not everybody is using them often. There are some conventional people who like the warmth of an adapted E-Mail and newsletters. Therefore, you need to know the needs of people and not just carelessly use the new tools. You can use the social media to influence where the power of internet marketing is building real personal relations and it is very important. This is as you are a human being and dealing with real people for whom relations become a matter.

What you need to know about social media marketing strategies:

- First of all, you need to know when it comes to set your strategy what will guide to your marketing promotion on social networking sites. This is one kind of plan that provides you the correct path; you need to follow to extend for acquiring as many business groups as possible and driving social media users for your old business website. The failure to has a well-known strategy to prepare for driving your campaign without anyway. You are not sure on how your marketing campaign will finish up.

- The development of an effective social marketing strategy is starting your social media marketing objective. Just, you will not be able to reach your marketing area deprived of establishing your goal. Your objective can make new leads by increasing followers on social networking sites, event advancement, drawing social media traffic to your outdated business website.

- The acute part of your marketing strategy must be used to grow any effort, your social media groups are used that have made in sharing your marketing posts. It is important that you hire a new way of growing your followers for their effort. You can use analytic tools and it would let you determine successful changes and income.

- A new serious part of your social marketing strategy would be how to measure your success. Marketing on social networking sites is not for the determination of making sales. This is as marketing on social media sites and also about social networking. The social media users certainly not visit the sites to shop for goods to connect with their friends. Your strategy would so aim at growing awareness about your business to your traditional business website.

- There are some ways by which you can successfully market your business on social media sites. Your employ would be one which is cost effective and very operative for getting your favorite results. You need to grow the fact that is raising an effective social marketing strategy to a big challenge when yours is a small business. The service of a social media marketing company becomes valuable. You need to assume careful look for the true company that is able to develop an effective marketing strategy though there are many such companies. By appealing the service of a company does not yet mean leaving the whole thing to the company. You choose to absorb in developing your strategy when you need to work firmly with a company.

Social media strategy for small business

The demand for online media has developed in now a day. This is both helping as a medium of contact and social communication. Online media are now helping as a stage for the small and middle scale inspirations to help their business and increase the brand visibility in the online sector. SMM or Social media marketing has formed an essential part of the small scale business. Social media marketing for small business houses has changed to become a remarkable formula that controls its success.

SMM facilities contain definite methods and well-expressed plans which will help a business website for better visibility and will give the web pages due contact. The demand for internet marketing is to optimize a website in the online domain. A number of methods are related to this and these services are recognized as social media optimization otherwise SMO service.

On the other hand, SMO contains all about e-marketing services for keeping a social community like building up online networks, blogs and forums, articles, video raise, and classified submission. It won't be wrong to say that SMO forms the most productive online marketing strategies and help the small businesses to increase projecting contact through the targeted set of audience.

SMM aids for small business which spread the essential information around a business's service to the set of targeted audience and in the method to help a visitor produce to be a potential buyer. So, we can say that online media marketing is both sizes the brand perception and provide correct contact to the businesses. It aids a business to make sales lead.

SMM for small scale business is riding an increase to the ladder in terms of efficiency and productivity with the rise of social networking websites. These social networking sites are providing a new aspect to online promotion services. Marketing and advertising by social networking sites are affordable and are the most widespread method of reaching out to a pool of audience.

Online media networks have allowed the small business houses to share and relate with the set of target audience and have paid greatly for dispersion of ideas and information with building brand consciousness. Social media optimization campaigns help to make a viral buzz in the online job. SMO movements are cheap ways where the reflectivity of the web page rises. The search engine positions of the websites improve as SMO services are inclined to bring tons of backlinks.

The strategy of social media marketing intended for small business would be suitable in order to make a business growing mass and popularity. The part is gaining fame with time and more global users. Small business holders can make recognized their range of goods and services. It is the time to extend bars for a good marketing experience if you have just started. One can correctly discover three things with prominent social media marketing activities. You need to turn on how well to produce. You will be conscious of the profit earning and you must know how to make popular applications.

1. **Letting business grow:** For a small business, the clutch attention is very essential for Social Media Marketing. The small businessperson can make the use of the PAT model for setting his efforts to support the business by successful media marketing. Planning and creating business are necessary if you want to enjoy success finally. You need to have things in place to make a small business run well. The establishing connection is very necessary. Networking is a vital point in making a business effective.

2. **Reaching out is a prime factor:** You have to take the real social media optimization services for globalizing business. By knowing in the group is the keyword to success. Try to make network through social media stages like Twitter and Facebook and talk about your business. The first work is to make a social interest among public. They would come and take a look at the method. They would recover to you through the same platform when they are converted the business is effective. Therefore, creating discussions is easy. The sort of social media marketing for small business is general. You should see how to design things and also extend to the maximum interested buyers and service workers.

3. **Making the bonding strong:** Social media marketing for small business is very effective for the handling of the tips. This might help you closing business deals in style. You should try to advertisement people of similar interest. It might be easy to form people attending worship. Be reliable as soon as interacting with the customers. You have to pay a high sum for the resolve when you are seen to be faked. An honest contact with the buyers will provide a way to long-standing relations.

4. **Forming the link:** It is essential to take the correct and familiar social media optimization services in trying to promote the popularity of your business. It would be the best if one can justify the process really in online. This might help you to make business popular over the modern technologies. You need

to talk about the products in details. When the customers ask queries about your definite products, try replying them in details about the basic points of great meaning. Though for the successful application of social media marketing for small business, the client bond would be appropriately related.

Chapter 4

Top 20 social media marketing tips

When you think about business, then you also need to think about marketing. Marketing is an essential part of your business and there are many ways to market and develop your business. You should be conscious of the popularity of the social networking sites. Social media provides different benefits to the followers. They provide a forum wherever you can interact with the public on many topics on your website. Social media marketing is the best things where you can sell your products.

You would have started with your marketing promotion at the end of the day. You would find that you are not receiving the effects as likely. Generally, this occurs when you lose out some important point. This is the cause why you would follow definite marketing tips.

These tips are really helpful to use social networking for business. First of all, you need to ask questions to the attentive visitors. You can involve your possible consumers with the help of these simple queries.

There is another social media marketing strategy that you need to follow having a correct posting plan. Your viewers will attract if you follow a plan for posting. You can use any of the social media sites like YouTube, Facebook or Twitter.

You can post at best once or twice each week to make interest. Many social media marketing tips can help you to become successful in business. Moreover, you can try to have a business for yourself that you can use on your business page.

The optimizing of your business page is very essential. You need to have social media expert all over the internet. It is always better to hire an expert when you are unable to plan the marketing strategies.

Here given below top 20 tips for social media marketing:

1. **Make Facebook account:** I think you know that Facebook tabs are the most important elements if you know a bit about Facebook marketing. Make certain that your Facebook visitors discover it easy to navigate over your custom tabs. There are many third-party apps that can help you to make contact with your visitors easier.

2. **Make a mobile-friendly blog:** There are many popular content management systems like WordPress that offer reactive websites to open like a dream at any desktop computer otherwise mobile device. Moreover, recent studies show that about 70% of Smartphone users want websites to load in 5 seconds. You need to consider the big time of your blog site to make certain that there is popular social sharing button combined on your blog site.

3. **Involve with nearby users:** The maximum advantage of using Tablets and Smartphones is that these devices can provide information made on a user's current position. So, users will find your business when they are searching for connected search questions. The best method to earn this benefit is by making location based on ads.

4. **Remove message fatigue:** Most of the Smartphone as well as Tablet users go for signals to get their social network informs. They only log off an account and login, not the same one. It is clear that your fans will get the same message constantly if you are posting the same message on all public networking websites. Sometimes, it may origin Message Fatigue. Thus, you need to make certain that your messages of tailor are only platforms to have the top return for your business.

5. **Use camera-dependent networks:** There are some social networks like Vine and Instagram that are designed mainly for mobile devices. Their progress relies wholly on Smartphones and Tablets and these networking websites are a fury these days. Therefore, you need to use these sites by taking photos and videos of your products and post them instantly. You will share your inside-story with your followers and provide them a chance to trust you.

6. **Twitter about your result to the world:** You can Tweet to update persons about your current and future cases. You would surround your content in such a way which it charms maximum readers' attention as Twitter lets only

140 characters in a single tweet. You would try to post however five tweets a day and do not forget to offer your event website link with every new tweet. You must tweet to all like-minded people to pull them to appear your event.

7. **Use of Google+ to the maximum extent:** Google+ is the modern networking use from Google. The event managers can use it to make an event buzz on the online social world. You can make an actions page on Google+ to share your program associated news and data with the target audience, use Circles to interact and share the news and data of the case within your group. Sometimes, Google Hangouts is used to start a video chat through your current and potential attendees.

8. **Create a company blog:** You need to make a company blog along with your own business website to progress photos and amazing articles on your future festivals and actions. You must hyperlink important keywords in your blog post to readers toward your company website.

9. **Use your LinkedIn profile:** LinkedIn is a common business networking site with a good amount of active users and uses this platform to inspire your potential attendees to give references on your profile. This stage is perfect for connecting with people of exact interests and business form. You can join many event groups and take part in their discussions. Moreover, you can submit links to these groups for new members to see.

10. **Comment on other's blog:** You must comment on others' blogs to increase the effect of your programs and make yourself suitable for the online viewers along with maintaining your own blog. You should read what others have to say about an article and try to comment on the same with a link.

11. **Use mobile phones to spread the word:** There are many online result management solutions where workers offer a natural mobile phone to send event related news to their target viewers through Smartphone. Moreover, you can send text messages to your consumers to inform them about your event's date and also time.

12. **Upload videos associated to your event on YouTube:** You can upload videos of your live events on YouTube. The people who are searching for events will come through your event videos and look out it. Moreover, you can link your video with the event registration to increase your ticket sales.

13. **Surveys your consumers:** You can use these sites to conduct proper surveys in order to discover what they think about your products. Facebook

fan page is good for creation a proper survey. Twitter can also be used to ask a question right about your brand.

14. **Monitor your consumers' opinions:** Realize what your consumers are talking about your brand to form YouTube comments otherwise Twitter tweets. These tools can be used by you like Social Mention to discover your consumer's sentiment about your products and services.

15. **Make your posts more applicable:** As soon as people started first by using the social sites, they were posting things like 'Going shopping with the kids.' The social sites have changed and developed. So, you need to start posting more applicable data. You should not make it to your readers and supporters only. You need to post solutions, motivation, and exciting evidence that can be suitable and helpful.

16. **Use features and tools:** The social sites are growing the capacities for your business using more tools and sorts than before. You need to take stock of all these tools and use them for the help of your followers and your business.

17. **Visual Marketing:** Sometimes, marketing is working visual and you need to do the same. Set in text and your business information in relevant graphics to post. Pinterest is the using of image sharing and has broken records through its development. Pictures are the commonly used and shared way of posting on Facebook. Once people share your images, you need them to see your website link.

18. **Help your clients:** You cannot offer solutions to all your consumers'. You should be willing to post links, data, and wealth of other businesses which can help your clients where you cannot.

19. **Host events:** You must hold regular events like clues, seminars, chats, networking parties, upgrades, etc. In recent times, Facebook has updated their event story and so it is cooler and more effective.

20. **Connections not sales:** You can use your social media pages to connect with your possible customers but not for sales. You need to use social media to share evidence, the answer to questions and comments. You do not need to bomb your social sites with sales fields and ads, help your followers to find solutions that do not pitch to them.

Chapter 5

Social media tips for small business

The current study shows that above half of small businesses trust in social media because it is an important marketing tool. Only 16% of those use their social media to talk directly with consumers. The common small business uses it in order to help as they use advertisements, direct mail and other kinds of marketing.

The using of social media for business development is very good. The actual leverage comes by appointment with people who are interested. Sometimes, your followers and fans are the actual catalysts for your success by using social media. Therefore, keeping in touch with them is acute.

Social media, like content marketing, is about building consumer relations. Actually, businesses can take their signal from the roots of social media such as a mainly 'social' tool. The sites like Facebook and Twitter were actually planned to help people for transferring information with each other, share assets and stay closely. Sometimes, businesses can do the same thing with their consumers by using the similar sites.

The using of social media sites is to employ with current and possible customers for taking a commitment of time. On the other hand, the tools are built in and so you can just imagine your company as a new method to connect with your target market, colleagues and relatives.

1. **Listen:** There are various discussions something like there. Among these, some of them can be about your company, your industry which affects you. You should take the time to listen what is being said earlier for determining how to reply it. You will learn new about what is essential to your target market.

2. **Take part:** You can show that you are attracted in what people have to say by becoming a suitable part of these conversations. Moreover, it is your chance to show how much you know about your subject. These subjects will help you to establish your authority. You should not be anxious to ask questions, inspire discussion and awaken some debate from time to time. It

helps people speaking and provides you more information to connect with them.

3. **Increase value:** Always your comments must add value to the conversation. If you are unable to add any valuable information and then you and your company will lose reliability. Imagine your efforts like a conversation before as a push for sales.

4. **Evaluate your aims:** First at the beginning of the way, you must think about your objects. After that, you will be able to achieve with your social media efforts. There are some businesses which want to raise brand realization; that interested in what their competitors are able to. By improving your primary aims will save your time and energy finally.

5. **Search the big picture:** You should think of social media as a community instead of a place to sell your products and also services. Just like the Internet generally, people on these sites are not certainly looking to buy somewhat. They want information as they are using, and they also want to connect with the sources for news. You should not lose sight of the information that you are to talk with people and offer them your skill, etc. You must design all individual post to make a general impress that returns your business purposes.

6. **Observer conversations:** There are some conversations that will happen on your Facebook page as well as other places wherever you must get warned to them. These will be easy to keep way but you need to make certain that you have a method of replying and comments both good and bad. In order to make the best use of the term of mouth natural surroundings like social media is very important.

7. **Get classified people's heads:** There are not exactly that would be incorrect. Just you need to work out where most of your clients are hanging out online and then make certain that you have a social media in those areas. This was not quite easy a few years ago because there weren't so many social media sites. But now there are many well separated: Facebook for customers, LinkedIn for business, Flickr for photo sharing and also a lot of social media. At present, the lines have become blurry; Pinterest is used to share photos and videos but these can show up on Facebook too. Customers can well find your name because the owner of the company contacts with you through LinkedIn.

8. **Keep things modern:** This is a bad knowledge for a potential client to acquire one of your social media goods, just to find that it looks like an online ghost town. It is a symbol that you don't actually care about your social media company if the last update was before. It is needed for you to diaries to keep posting to any of the social media that you use on an even source. You need to make certain that all the several places you use for social media are kept up to date as you should keep your personal website often updated. With the messages which are tailored for your individual social media site before sent out as an automatic 'one size fits all' flash to all the different sites.

Thus, when you are thinking about using social media to improve your business, think of to put some time into customer appointment. It is the best method to get those friends and fans to convert into consumers.

Process of getting success in social media marketing for small business

There are many entrepreneurs and advertisers who fail to achieve the chosen result when selecting for social media marketing for small businesses. Here are given some tips to stop the risk of these marketing failures:

- You should not abuse the power of optimization. If you improve your content to use the search engine results, many search engines can block it. If you do the actual search engine optimization, sooner or later your search engine rankings will develop.
- You must increase your social network by connecting to related business website pages. Find websites that offer products and services to balance your offering. Exchange website links and helps each other's business from strategic unions.
- As soon as you make your profile on social networking sites, provide a link to your "About Us" page rather than "Home Page". This might provide information where visitors desire to know when they visit your website.
- You should not use more time on advertising than the quality of the content which you post on websites. You need not try hard to develop your business

if you provide effectively and keyword rich content as your content will do this job.

Some businesses like restaurants and clubs seem a natural apt for social media. The active online company is a great method to get your consumers to charm their friends by social media sites like Facebook and Twitter. There are many ways of social media that can add value to your business if your company does not appear like a clear fit. Here are five simple tips on getting started:

1. Start small: You should not need to make an account on every social media site. Think about your consumers' use which fits your business. For big destinations Foursquare is very useful, Twitter rapidly can help to get news and updates your followers. Facebook is perfect for building community and distribution tips and advice. You can pick the one which supports your business and start with that. You can add extra accounts and link them to increase your presence.

2. Use control: This is easy to get happy about the potential to connect with all your customers and views when you get started with social media. You must not spoil it and your labors failure. Show some limitation and tweet when you have rather useful to say. You will want to post or tweet once a week.

3. Become applicable: When you have some good tips that are related to your business, share them. You would want to have special reasons for your groups. You must turn over what interests your customers. They must not want to be bombed with positive messages and valuable info is always loved. You would provide offers on how to keep pets happy and healthy when their owners are away if you are a pet babysitter.

4. Keep it brief: It is not needed for you to write a novel to be effective with social media. When your message is small, it will be read and one valuable trick when drafting a message to write what you want to say. Then return over your draft to cut words that you do not actually need. By making your message more concise and prevailing, any fluff and filler words must go.

5. Grow personal: Some people like to know there is a human heart after the companies do business. It is mainly important to confined businesses. Presenting your character in your posts makes them more motivating to read for customers. It does not mean to share the whole thing. On the other hand, an informal tone with a small number of interesting scraps about your hobbies, pets, loves and hates makes your business friendlier.

Chapter 6

Importance of social networking in business

What is a social network?

Social networking is reflected like a platform by which social relations will be made between people and information sharing will be enabled. Personal information and relations can be shared as well as users can stay in touch by social networks sites.

The most of the SNSs offer a personal page for posting, the capacity to search for friends and other matters like improving the profile and particular data and the skill is to keep the stated information by page owner from the eyes of the public.

These Online services have enhanced the actions of persons on online jobs, mainly in the point of social networks for the determination of preserving friendships irrespective of distance. It allows people to get better jobs and partners.

Regarding the acceptance of these sites by people, companies have become elaborate to get involved in this method though they can sell their products and services. The better work consumer's needs and wants to the inquiry of customer buying forms and their feedbacks they can fine tune their result making procedure along with their strategies.

Importance of social networking

If you are a new mother who needs to stay at home and spend some time with your family lacking of sacrificing your economic liberty, a home business is a solution for you. By creation, a home business provides you the liberty of selecting your working hours and costs value time to your children. At that time, you need to confirm that the business is effective.

You need to know the importance of social networking to see your home-business show. Really, the social network is a social building that is created by persons and organizations who share mutual business welfares. The importance of social networking lies in the element where you can connect with people who can become your future customers in time. The importance of social networking is being understood by gradual work from home mothers.

You are certainly going to try for making your business success to continue to remain at home. Social networking can certainly help you when you are trying to extend new views and spread your market. Therefore, recognize the importance of networking. You are confirming to provide the best home business for understanding the importance of networking to confirm a turnkey to rich bonuses.

The importance of social networking lies in the cool methods to link the people to you and there are many sites offering free membership which again does your job without any cost. For this, you can make a social networking page of your own create quality business and it is absolutely free. The linking of people and collecting information are also the causes that add the importance of networking.

A different benefit of networking is that it can be completed from the warm comforts of your home and this improves great value to your home business when you spoil your children. You need to discover the online societies of organizations common events, securities, and obviously business ideas. Most web-based networking sites offer many ways to connect with the users at low costs which would be beneficial for you. The main importance of networking is that businesses run generally, social networks make it simpler the process by making it easier to reach the contacts around the world.

When building relations with the online communities, you need to keep in mind the following things:

- **Select words wisely:** It is wise to choose your words as generally you will not be more aware of others on the site. You should not ever know who can unexpectedly insult for using tact and do not offer your views except asked.

This code of conduct is suggested as soon as you are in an environment wherever you have established yourself.

- **Be hopeful:** The most actual methods to build relations are to build people by being positive and offering help. By acting in this system makes you more friendly and pretty to others and it is just what you want when social network marketing.

- **Share industry tips and update:** It is a very sensitive manner of building reliability when filtering out those who can have an attention in what you work. You are about to share by offering a link and thus, people can find out more by posting your messages which easily turns into the information. Though, care needs to be taken here by not let this for any kind of updating to control your discussions as remembering on a social site.

- **From your specialist:** You should not swagger into any discussion saying your expert as you will repel others. It is not rather than you can do but it is made by becoming a dependable source for news and information. It is proposed for you to build your authority in a more sensitive way by sharing some information if they select. Social network marketing is hooked on your reliability and so be sure that your share is correct.

- **Mix it up:** You will experience the best success in social network marketing by keeping a regular guy. You must show your social side by donating to current debates and try to lend price too. It will make your aids be obvious when making a more influence with others. Mistake your advertising action with your amusing labors, and by the by if you find socializing an effort, it can be time to clear for a while. You can enjoy your experience as it is what these sites are bound for.

When a firm code of activities is preserved by the individual marketer, social networking for business is the most actual. This is essential to gather these sites were not going to commerce than casual gatherings. So, social network marketing is the first order for a business to create relationships instantly. When you hope to skill positive earnings from your social network marketing efforts, your own conduct will play a main role.

Benefits social networking for business

The social networking for business is mainly on the internet for providing some extreme welfare when it is completed properly. Social networking is suitable, fun and permits you to cover many grounds from correct before your computer. The benefits you stand to increase much deeper to help your business and at a faster rate. Actually, there can be no more amusing method to increase your online presence than by your mixing with others on the internet.

Here is given some important methods to build your business by socializing at these networking sites.

- **Builds brand consciousness:** Online social networking is the best stage for increasing a brand and can be done easily. This is able to maintain a reliability in your words and activities which will help to develop and support the identity of your selecting.
- **Goes viral:** The people start from many social sites and come from different experiences and grip variable interests. Taking their care with so forth, it can be that you signify these people and can take this information and share it with their friends. This viral result is a great and very effective method to build your business online.
- **Efficiency:** This is the power of working within these community sites to help your goods and facilities. It is possible for people presenting you to their friends if you are found interesting enough. You are increasing your online company in this way and giving you greater positive potential down the line. These new links signify new channels where you can present any goods and services.
- **Increases marketing efficiency:** You are really taking steps which will increase your marketing efficiency as it is suggested to make friends formerly trying to promote anything in any social community. The fact is that people are more likely to do business with you if they are familiar with you as this increases the faith they feel.

Social networking for business is a great system to influence your efforts as soon as you build your business on the internet. Beating into the fame of online social networking sites can let you increase your online presence and offers other important benefits as reviewed above. On behalf of any hopeful internet entrepreneur which is short on assistance but long on wish by using social sites to build your business.

Chapter 7

Ways to use social media for business

The using of social media for business has become popular to change with the use of the internet. There has been not anything like social media earlier of the Internet for business marketing. This is one kind of trend where all modern businesses must take into thought as part of their positive system and as a mode of advertising. The world of client service and open communication has been improved by the start of social networks. It can become the favorite way of communication with users of all types.

Social Marketing is using the online social networks to develop and promote a company to customers. The customers can become cooperating with the businesses as they use by fan pages and linking to blogs through the social networks. There are many social networks to businesses that are the most suitable way to contact information among each other. Social networks help consumers feel and also they are getting a more personal communication with the companies over social media communication.

Social media marketing permits for much faster communication among companies and their customers and it lends itself to a wider base of potential customers from their friend's networks. This lets companies promote with a small investment and is the most cost effective method to help any current online business. It is assumed in companies, independent businesses, and even home businesses.

Use of online communication by social media is the modern trend in advertising for companies above the world. Now, small businesses can contest for their market with bigger companies and they can do it without having vast quantities of capital for advertising finances. It is considered as a great equalizer in the current information age and social media is producing a revolution in the way companies do business. There is anyone who has a modern company must take benefit of social media.

The using of social media for business can change the method of the modern company that uses the Internet and can change the way customer service is controlled. The customer can cooperate with modern company's right that makes their experience more personal. This will be able to make a lasting impress on the modern customer and make a link with them. It will also help to keep them coming back to the company that delivers them top quality customer service.

Here described some ways to use social media for your Internet marketing efforts:

1) Become active in Facebook groups: The best ways to build your online business is by creating relations with others who are acquiring success online. The best method to do this is by becoming active in groups they have taking place.

Do what you can to assurance on the individual and the products they sell in your motion in these groups. Sometimes, they will take the sign of your support, and when you attitude them with some opinions and ideas, they will be open to forming a relation with you. This relation can profit you a lot over time.

2) Use the Twitter "search" purpose: Twitter search function works nearly as a 'lead search,' because you will be able to catch people who are talking about things which relate to the areas of emphasis on your site. It will be able to connect with them at their point of want.

When you are running an affiliate website for digital cameras to catch people on Twitter by asking questions about buying a digital camera, there is an opportunity for you to make a link with them at their point of need and bring them to your site.

3) Build your platform: Facebook and Twitter can help you to build your platform because you can set up yourself as an expert in your area of social media. The more you are able to build your status as an expert and the more profits you will make online. These tips will help you to deal with using social media to lead your success online.

4) Choose and perform your strategy correctly: You will find many ways to use social media to market a business. You must select the most suitable and most actual ones. You need to select the strategy where you will actually get support to your business and also to use this process properly to achieve the best results. You will easily overcome when you try to do too many things. Therefore, concentrate on a single aim and finally, you shall achieve your primary objective.

5) Plan your actions: By planning the results that you have made about your social media actions and that is a certain efficient method to excel in this kind of marketing. You need to have a planning calendar wherever you can put all of your events, and the accounts that you are using in posting.

The social media calendar is one kind of planning tool as it will help you to form your social activities and so you can bring your marketing message obviously to your followers. You will see the exact topics and subjects which you must cover when you have filled the calendar with all your deeds for marketing and advertising works that you need to start. You should make assured that all of the things that you issued can be made, shared, followed and achieved to exploit their experience.

6) Monitor your results: You performed the plan to keep an eye on your results, monitor the results and work out what they mean for your business. A calendar is an exceptional tool for pursuing your metrics for the whole year. It will help to keep scores of some statistics that can help you to fix which campaign is working as well as which one is not. You must check and examine these results that you are receiving from social media; they will also help you to modify your plans and to enhance your campaigns.

Chapter 8

Social media marketing companies

The facilities of a social media marketing company are charming very much now a day. Social media publicity has improved by controlling the internet world. The social media sites like Twitter and Facebook are controlling millions of computers and mobile phones. Users of these sites are not impartial for looking the information. They are keenly talking about many issues and interests. It is sure that millions of users offer a useful audience for promoting products and services of businesses.

Many social media marketing companies claim to offer exceptional services. As you will be capitalizing your hard-earned money, time and work, you need to select one that will really help your business aims. You need to confirm that you are working for a very responsible company which will be your partner in your future activities. You must make certain that the companies will not compromise your success. Here are given some issues which you need to consider when selecting to hire a social media marketing company.

- **Reputation:** The reputable social media company does not have to sales by talking only their method but they do it by receiving your belief. The company through a good name has taken many businesses to success. This has brought excellent services to their customers. The company is very suggested by your colleagues.

- **Years of service:** The good social media marketing companies have years of skill in the industry of providing services. They have been confirmed and verified to provide good service. They have a skilled and qualified staff working for them and have been about for years in spite of the challenges in the useful market. They know how to cross above coarse tides and coasts. Moreover, they used advanced methods to confirm that you are always a step in front of your competitors.

- **Validity:** Most of the time, good social media marketing companies are valid. There is one shot of the boom of online business and that is the vast blast of scammers who will use scheme and steal to get their dirty hands interested in your hard earned money. Select one which is reliable and proven by other clients and that has established good reviews.

- **Flexibility:** The good social media marketing companies are flexible to provide the range of needs of your customers. They will offer an exact business plan of action for your specific business according to wants and aims. Besides, they offer flexible payment system that is satisfactory to your case. Make assured they provide a payment system which will confirm success on their end and on yours too.

Advantages of hiring a social media marketing company

The social media marketing companies can offer you the skilled service that is chosen to support your business. You would not feel the need of an extra hand if you have a small business. You can dream of what the top of the tools and methods from these activities which can carry to your business. They might help you to increase your business and develop your success.

They can help to save you time and work by doing most of the job. Similarly, they base their plan and activities on consistent record to confirm that your advertisements reach to a correct target. They will make certain to employ the real marketing procedures and junk the ones that do not work. They will be capable of adjusting their plans directly to the changes in the market. They will be ready in cases of tests that lie fast with their highly trained staff and you have sufficient time to spend on other activities like doing administrative tasks to promote the development of your business. You have more time for other areas of your business which need your highest attention.

They are very profitable. You are assured to gain the maximum profits with the excellent service of the company when you spend money to hire a social media marketing company. Your profit of funds will make hiring an agency for your while.

Chapter 9

How to increase social network

The social networks have increased over the last year or so happening out as a few lists to try and acquire in touch with old friends who has grown into a multi-million dollar industry. The trouble is that they are as valuable as their owners suggest of the present day wherever computers and mobiles phones are taking over so much of our lives, deprived of giving much back in return.

It is very easy to forget social networks because just another time-wasting action of kids and youths by spending uncountable hours talking nonsense and small talk till the early hours are using their computers. Though, they are as essential a part of current communications as the phone was half a century before.

In a perfect world that is probably the target of social networks and they will be an outstanding medium for people to meet and socialize out of their working situation for whatever purpose of any other socializing work. Then there is a hidden power which will be soon sensitive that will be a help to keep a quickly growing economy.

There is a market for a product in any economy, and there are customers of those products. You can see how efficient marketing based economy and might work if it were to be possible to have a real process of describing all products and services with a similar table of prepared customers.

We have a condition where there are an increasing number of social networks to somebody only for socializing and almost like time satisfying for children, and others for users without time to kill. A growing number of others is to make a supplier to customer role, and yet others who make a business to business part.

The secret is to be capable of identifying from the growing excess of social networks because one falls into the group. You can select the wrong one, and whatnot you might hope to reach by using that site will be wholly wasted.

Selecting the correct one to meet your real needs is very essential. You would be able to direct your bulletins to a clearly recognized market and marketing on such sites would be targeted that marketing would return very high returns on your investment.

There is a power of social networks and its power is to spread the word virally. Not like sales like email and it might take only one pleased consumer to write a short review on his social network. At that time, this person can have 47 other contacts, and some of those can have thousands, and thus the message would use to send thousands upon thousands of contacts.

In an age of wholly changing buying habits and then social networks can aid many suppliers to overcome the problems of buyers to remove from conventional shopping and more on-line customer outlets.

Fast tips to increase social network traffic

- You need to start a weekly blog.
- Provide your users pretty and besides a sales pitch to read in order to give them the aim to remember your name.
- Try to keep it short, no more than a page in a word text.

- Use paragraphs and makes your point to a valid blog post, not a 30 second used car commercial.
- Improve weekly if not daily
- Save your content fresh if you refresh your rank daily, keep things moving.
- Make discussions and let users interact

Chapter 10

Advantages of social media for business

The business creativities cannot ever terminate the influence of the online communities being the platform which help them increasing well contact and improve their brand visibility. Online media has become a great method of reaching to the possible consumers in most efficient and cost real method. The online communities, mainly the social networking websites have thousands of listed users and are rising all day. Facebook registers more than a million of memberships. There are about more than a lac of tweets appearing on Twitter every day. The communities as MySpace have above a 100 million users internationally. These social media sites are using a tool by the business house to platform their service without troubles. So, it is not a wrong idea to support that social optimization for business has been the most surprising revolution that connects their development in most actual methods.

Social media on behalf of business has a lot of advantages and the main one is that it lets you extend to a large set of online viewers base. Get in touch with online societies and cooperate with a large number of probable customers. The advertising in online societies means that the online consumers can have reached you with the greatest ease. Social networking provides the chance for you to give a fast reply to your clients. The key thing which is essential in SMM service is correct strategy and good planning.

Online communication is simple and costs effective in Social media for business. By following the simple SMM services, the business houses can provide good results in terms of reflectivity and existence in the domain. The social marketing campaigns like e-mail campaigning can demand the clients and the newsletter campaigns allow the possibility of turning a simple visitor into a buyer.

A lot of online users denote the social people and websites to catch reviews about a specific service provider. So, posting reviews is a different good method to appeal visitors to your site. SMM contains social media optimization facilities that play a vital role in product or business upgrade.

Social optimization facilities contain a range of promotional program that contains article and press release submission, networking with the online viewers by joining in the discussion forums and loads of other mess. SMO service purposes at making correct brand consciousness and aiming full traffic to the client's websites.

The social marketing for business includes some applications which are intended to draw different online users. The services are reduced by an SMM emphasis on online brand improvement strategies. These companies express the exact social media rules and help you with a different method that will help your business carve a separate niche.

The top rank in search engine pages help a business to gain qualified contact, but there are certainly other important issues related to it. Social media optimization facilities have grown to deliver the great result to the business enterprises to the extent that their web visibility is concerned. You need to be aware of the goal that you wish to realize over SMM and over strategic method as a business owner. It is a matter of time that your business will love more credit online.

Here given two advantages of social media marketing:

- Social media lets you reach much wider viewers than old offline methods of marketing. Thus, before spending hours upon hours joining networking actions in your local area, you can use Twitter's file and follow and cooperate with local companies which you must like to do business in a very time-saving method.
- While offline methods of marketing like flyers, pictures, and journal and newspaper ads are very detached from your viewers, you have no control as they read your pretty leaflet; social media allows you to really cooperate with a vast amount of people. There is not anything incorrect about tweeting

to somebody, you have never met before where some people discover it very difficult to approach at a networking occurrence.

Disadvantages of social media marketing

- When you 'post' rather you did not mean to say and it does not matter how fast you remove it, many people will have seen it as so many people have profiles on these social media and you will degrade yourself before thousands instead of just a couple of people.

- When you are not careful about how you use your social networking profiles for expert 'friends' who maybe see the things that you would be a drunken chat between you and a friend who would not be fit for the office. Then, it is the best to have two profiles, a business, and personal one though these can be very dull to manage.

Conclusion

Thank you again for downloading this book!

I hope this book was able to help you to know about social media marketing and how can you use social media for your business purpose to earn more profit.

To the end, if you enjoyed this book, please take the time to share your thoughts and post a review. It'd be greatly respected!

Thank you and good luck!

www.ingramcontent.com/pod-product-compliance
Lightning Source LLC
Chambersburg PA
CBHW080528190526
45169CB00008B/3095